More Animal
JOKES
A Buddy Book
by U.R. Phunny
Buddy BOOKS
More Jokes!

VISIT US AT

www.abdopub.com

Published by ABDO Publishing Company, 4940 Viking Drive, Suite 622, Edina, Minnesota 55435.

Printed in the United States.

Edited by: Sarah Tieck
Contributing Editors: Jeff Lorge, Michael P. Goecke
Graphic Design: Deborah Coldiron
Illustrations by: Deborah Coldiron and Maria Hosley

Library of Congress Cataloging-in-Publication Data

Phunny, U.R., 1970-
More animal jokes / U.R. Phunny.
p. cm. — (More jokes!)
Includes Index.
ISBN 1-59197-872-6
1. Animals—Juvenile humor. 2. Riddles, Juvenile. I. Title. II. Series.

PN6231.A5P54 2005
818'.5402—dc22

2004057519

How does a lobster get from place to place?

By taxi-crab!

What's worse than raining cats and dogs?

Hailing taxi cabs!

What do dogs eat at the movie theater?

Pup-corn!

What do you get when you cross a dog with an elephant?

A very nervous postman!

What pet makes the loudest noise?

A trum-pet!

What happened when 500 hares got loose on the main street?

The police had to comb the area!

What do giraffes have that no other animal has?

Baby giraffes!

At what time does a duck wake up?

At the quack of dawn!

What do you give an elephant with big feet?

Plenty of room!

What says, "Quick! Quick!"?

A duck with hiccups!

What do you get if you cross a cat with a dog?

An animal that chases itself!

What do penguins eat for lunch?

Iceberg-ers!

How do you get a mouse to smile?

Say cheese!

How does a turkey eat its food?

It gobbles it up!

How should you treat a baby goat?

Like a kid!

What did the bat say to his Valentine?

I love hanging around you!

Where do frogs take notes?

On lily pads!

Why did the frog eat a lamp?

Because he wanted a light snack!

What do cats call their grandfather?

Grand-paw!

What do you get when you cross a snake and a kangaroo?

A jump rope!

What did Leonardo da Vinci's cow paint?

The MOO-na Lisa!

What do you call a dancing sheep?

A BAA-lerina!

Why are cats good at video games?

Because they have nine lives!

What day of the week do chickens hate?

Fry-day!

What's it called when a cat sues another cat?

A claw-suit!

Why are skunks so smart?

Because they have a lot of scents!

Where did the duck go when he was sick?

To the duck-tor!

What do frogs drink at parties?

Croak-a-cola!

What did the little chicken say to the bully?

Peck on someone your own size!

What do you call a chicken from outer space?

An egg-straterrestrial!

What has two humps and is found at the North Pole?

A lost camel!

What do you get when you cross a pig and a teddy bear?

A teddy boar!

Why aren't elephants allowed on beaches?

They can't keep their trunks up!

Customer: How much is that duck?
Shopkeeper: Ten dollars.
Customer: Okay, could you please send me the bill?

Shopkeeper: I'm sorry, but you'll have to take the whole bird!

What do you get if you cross a cat with a parrot?

A carrot!

What do you call a sheep that is always quiet?

A SHHHH-eep!

Why do baby birds say, "Cheep, cheep, cheep"?

Because they can't say, "Expensive, expensive, expensive!"

What's a paw-paw?

A puppy's foot-foot!

What do you get if you cross a crocodile with a flower?

I don't know, but I'm not going to smell it!

What goes "tick, tick, woof, woof"?

A watch dog!

What do you call a sleeping bull?

A bull-dozer!

What do cats eat for breakfast?

Mice Crispies!

What do you get if you cross a sheepdog and a flower?

A collie-flower!

Who tells the best chicken jokes?

Comedi-hens!

What's the difference between a man and a dog?

One wears a suit and the other just pants!

Why couldn't the dalmatian hide?

He was already spotted!

Why don't anteaters get sick?

Because they are full of ant-ibodies!

What happened to the dog that swallowed a firefly?

It barked with de-light!

What do you get if you cross a cocker spaniel with a poodle and a rooster?

A cockapoodledoo!

Visit ABDO Publishing Company on the World Wide Web. Joke Web sites for children are featured on our Book Links page. These links are monitored and updated to provide the silliest information available.

www.abdopub.com